The Downing Street Guide to Party Etiquette

Praise

'Verity Bigg-Knight has written a . . . book.'
– *Ipswich Pedant*

'It is truly amazing that this was published.'
– *Bullfighting Weekly*

'Darling, I don't have time to read this. Just let me know how much you need for next month.'
– Sir Adrian Bigg-Knight

The Downing Street Guide to Party Etiquette

VERITY BIGG-KNIGHT

WILDFIRE

About the Author

Verity Bigg-Knight was born in Kensington in 1988. Her father is Sir Adrian Edgcumbe Miles Bigg-Knight, 2nd Baronet, but that doesn't mean she didn't work really hard for everything she has. She attended St Hortensia's School for Sociable Girls before reading History of Art at the University of Bridgeford (she got a third, which was actually impressive, given her best mate, Tuffy Lloyd-George, broke her leg skiing a week before exams). During her time at uni, she threw many widely praised bashes, including a 'pimps and hos' party so convincing it was shut down by the Met's Vice Unit.

Upon graduating, she set up a company, Verity's Large Evenings, with nothing but her own blood, sweat and tears (plus a £2 million loan from Daddy). This bespoke party-planning service has been tremendously successful: its clients include Princess Eugenie, Mumford & Sons and half the cast of *Made in Chelsea*. Her events boast a diverse range of guests, from businessmen to businessmen's wives, Etonians to Harrovians, billionaires to only-just-millionaires. Verity is also a committed activist for social justice, frequently sharing woke infographics on Instagram. Her dream is to start a foundation to teach underprivileged kids the correct pronunciation of wines.

The Downing Street Guide to Party Etiquette is her first book (written, not read).

First published in 2022 by
WILDFIRE
an imprint of HEADLINE PUBLISHING GROUP

First published in paperback in 2023 by
WILDFIRE
an imprint of HEADLINE PUBLISHING GROUP

1

Cataloguing in Publication Data is available from the British Library

ISBN 978 1 0354 1056 9

Illustrations by Eva Bee

Designed and typeset by EM&EN
Printed and bound in Great Britain by Clays Ltd, Elcograf S.p.A.

Headline's policy is to use papers that are natural, renewable and recyclable
products and made from wood grown in well-managed forests and other
controlled sources. The logging and manufacturing processes are expected
to conform to the environmental regulations of the country of origin.

HEADLINE PUBLISHING GROUP
An Hachette UK Company
Carmelite House
50 Victoria Embankment
London EC4Y 0DZ

www.headline.co.uk
www.hachette.co.uk

Acknowledgements

It's not easy being a party planner *cum* socialite: the stress of hosting, the constant travel, the repetitive strain injuries from lifting champagne flutes. These hardships take a toll over the years, so you need friends and acquaintances of the highest calibre. I've been super lucky in that respect. Big-time thanks to Mimsy Terfington-Gulch, Angus Chicken-McNugget, Demeter Crosby-Stills, Jemima Nash-Young, Heloise Gorst-Pendejo, Zara Primark-Benetton, Lucinda Waitrose-Ocado, Hugo and Olly Bultitude, Mimi Van Hogendorp, Tallulah Cuthbertson-Wang, Esmerelda 'Twink' Fortescue, Tabbs Granger-O'Brien-Dunt, Ziggy Al-Rashid, Morton Frisbee, Count Otto Friedrich Jägersbacher, Pyramus Dalrymple, Rufus Proudbottom and Iain Charmander-Squirtle. Without their kindness and wisdom, this book wouldn't be half as good as I imagine it is.

I'm indebted to my circle of close pals, Tashy, Bingles, Minch, Fup-Fup, Zarbo, Gonky, Squnk and The Lasho-saurus. Thanks are also due to Pandora Nepotism-Case, the most talented writer I know, who read my manuscript and declined to give any notes, saying there was, I quote, 'no point'. High praise indeed!

And, finally, the couple without whom this book would never have happened: Boris and Carrie.

Disclaimer

The following is entirely fictional. In no way does the author mean to suggest that parties took place in Downing Street during lockdown, or that those working there broke the rules, knowingly or otherwise.

Unrelated Quotes

'The event lasted for a number of hours. There was excessive alcohol consumption by some individuals. One individual was sick. There was a minor altercation between two other individuals.'

The Sue Gray report

'Best of luck – a complete non story but better than them focusing on our drinks (which we seem to have got away with)'

WhatsApp message sent by Martin Reynolds, principal private secretary to Boris Johnson, referring to the Downing Street garden party on 20 May 2020

CONTENTS

—◆—

INTRODUCTION

———◆———

According to *The Oxford English Dictionary*, the definition of 'party' is:

1. *a social gathering of invited guests, typically involving eating, drinking and entertainment.*

And:

2. *a formally constituted political group that contests elections and attempts to take part in government.*

Someone who knows a great deal about both types of party is Boris Johnson. Our prime minister (former prime minister? I don't follow the news) has always loved a good knees-up, from his time wrecking restaurants in the Bullingdon Club to getting wrecked himself at the Italian castle of billionaire Evgeny Lebedev. With Boris in Number Ten, it could be said that PM now stands for 'Party Monster'. And why shouldn't he let his flaxen hair down? Our ruling class need some kind of relief valve. I mean, imagine how stressful it is being in charge of the UK. You have to visit godforsaken places like Luton and pretend to care what normal people think.

As the reader may recall, reports began to circulate in late November 2021 of a series of gatherings in Downing

Street. These had taken place during strict public-health restrictions due to a little something that rhymes with 'novel boronavirus'. Soon enough, the British people were in an uproar: 'How could you do this while we were locked down? How could you flout the very rules you imposed on all of us? How could you endanger the population, given the disease was ripping through care homes and vaccines weren't available?' Blah blah blah.

Eventually, I realised why there had been such furore around so-called Partygate: the British public were jealous that they weren't invited. They wished they could have been at these cool, glamorous soirées, shoulder to shoulder with civil servants and Tory special advisers. That's when the idea for this book took shape. I'm a top-class party planner, used to mixing with society's *crème de la crème*.* If I shared the benefit of my years of experience, then anyone – no matter how povvo or gross – could enjoy the most fabulous parties. It would be my gift to the unwashed masses (provided they stump up £12.99 RRP). This dream has now come true. You hold in your hands the ultimate guide to saying 'pandemic, schmandemic' and partying down in Downing Street.

'But, Verity,' I hear you say, 'what's the point of this book, when I don't even work in Downing Street?' Well, first of all: rude. Secondly, there are myriad lessons the average

---

* Famous brain-box Stephen Fry once called me 'jejune', a pretty word I must look up some day.

reader can glean, even if they subsist on a mere six figures, or live somewhere dreadful like Hull. Sure, the following pages make reference to prestigious institutions, famed buildings and powerful personages. But, with a bit of imagination, it should be clear how this translates to your bedsit/squat/hovel. When I say 'Waitrose', think 'Lidl'. When I say 'Chancellor of the Exchequer', think 'your mate Baz'. When I say 'Dominic Cummings', think 'your weirdest uncle'.

If you take one thing from my book, let it be this: you don't need to be prime minister to throw a Downing Street party. Downing Street parties are a state of mind, one that says, 'Sod the pandemic, I want to crack open an M&S mojito and get stuck into a Colin the Caterpillar cake.' Any time you prioritise your whims over the lives of others, that's a Downing Street party. Any time you choose to get smashed in the office until 3am instead of going home to your family, that's a Downing Street party. And any time you display total contempt for the intelligence of your fellow countrymen and women, that's a Downing Street party. The only rule is: the rules are subject to interpretation.

So read on, and let's party like it's 2020!

Socially distanced hugs and kisses,

V. Bigg-Knight

GETTING READY

INVITATIONS

—◆—

Invitations are an essential component of any party. A party without invitations will likely consist of you sitting alone, sipping a bottle of Heineken and watching the guacamole turn brown. On the flip side, invitations without a party will lead to a crowd of thwarted revellers and, quite possibly, violence. This rule can be simply expressed as an equation:

$$INVITATIONS + PARTY = SUCCESS^*$$

However, before sending out invites, you need to ask yourself a fundamental question: should I be having a party in the first place? The answer, invariably, is yes. There's never a bad time to throw caution to the wind, pop on your glad rags and boogie down. That goes double when you're working in Number Ten, and quadruple during a pandemic.

Some people will tell you it's never appropriate to hold a mass gathering in the midst of a national lockdown. These are what we in the trade refer to as 'poopers'. Pay them no heed. As the Beastie Boys once observed, you gotta fight for your right to party.

---

* I got a D in GCSE Maths, but I'm pretty sure this checks out.

To invite or not to invite,
that is the question.

W. Shakespeare
paraphrased by V. Bigg-Knight

Now that you've decided to go ahead with the event, novel coronaviruses be damned, your next task is to draw up a guest list. Party invitations are always political, and especially so when you work in politics. This is a guide to who should be rewarded and who should be brutally snubbed.

INVITATION WORTHINESS CALCULATOR

Hard-working colleague –
ADD 5 POINTS.

Personally loyal –
ADD 10 POINTS.

Related to someone on the *Sunday Times* Rich List –
ADD 15 POINTS.

Attractive and potentially willing to have sex with you –
ADD 20 POINTS.

Able to advance/protect your career –
ADD 100 POINTS.

Already knows the party is happening and could dob you in to the press –
ADD 200 POINTS.

A nice person who is pleasant to be around –
IRRELEVANT, ZERO POINTS.

Okay, time to tot up the score . . .

LESS THAN 20 POINTS: Wallflower alert! This nerd isn't worth inviting to a Zoom event – on no account should they be allowed near your party. What would the cool kids think?

20–100 POINTS: Okay, they may not be the life and soul, but this person has something to bring to the table. Invite them at your discretion, though perhaps let them know that they only just made the grade.

100 POINTS PLUS: Total legend. You need them at your party: secure their attendance by any means necessary. Not only should you invite them to the main do, but also the afterparty in the PM's residence.

Of course, you can't be totally political – you're not some monster, devoid of human feeling. There will naturally be some people so important to you that it doesn't matter if they meet the above criteria. For instance, the high-priced decorator currently doing up your flat. Feel free to drop them an invite, even if it undermines your defence that these get-togethers are essential government work.

FORMALITY

The level of formality you employ in your invitation lets prospective guests know what they can expect at the party itself. Here are some examples, ranging from most to least formal:

1) *9 × 6-inch card, eggshell white, embossed with your family crest. Your name and details engraved; your guest's name written in finest calligraphy*

LORD AND LADY EXAMPLETON

request the pleasure of the company of

Blanky McBlank

at their home on Thursday, 32nd Febtember

RSVP

50 Grosvenor Crescent, SW1X   Drinks   7:30–9:30

2) *Email with specially designed banner featuring balloons*

Hi Blanky,

Just to let you know, we're having a little get-together at our place next Thursday. We'll be breaking out the bubbly around half seven, but you can turn up whenevs. We'd be absolutely effing <u>delighted</u> if you could make it. Hit us back when you get the chance.

Much love,

Rubastian and Tashmantha

3) *Text*

mate. major pissfest 2nite. u in?

> **TOP TIP**
>
> Invites can also be an excellent weapon of psychological warfare. Just go up to your office enemy and, with a flourish, give them a golden invitation card. Then freeze and, with a feigned expression of horror, say, 'Oh, God, I'm so sorry: that's actually meant for X.' Take the invite from your enemy and hand it to whoever works next to them.

HOW TO WRITE A CODED INVITATION

While you can't have a party without invitations, you might not want your illicit event to leave a paper trail. Perhaps you're a well-known figure with an important job, say one that sounds like 'Bime Finister'. In that case, you should craft an invite with plausible deniability. Here is a glossary of code words and phrases that can be used to conceal the nature of your gathering:

Wild piss-up	Important governmental business
Wine	Policy juice
Blasting Spotify's This is ABBA playlist at full volume	Cultural exchange with the people of Sweden
Shouting match	Frank debate over ideas
Drunken brawl	Robust debate over ideas
Photocopying your arse	Workplace-mandated medical examination

To help you further, here's an example of a super-subtle invitation:

> Dear colleague with whom my interactions are exclusively professional,
>
> I hereby invite you to an IMPORTANT MEETING in the basement at 5pm on Tuesday. There will be <u>intoxicating</u> discussion of legislative priorities, and a <u>song and dance</u> will be made about policy reform. These discussions may go on until the wee hours. BYOB (Bring Your Own Briefcase).
>
> Yours soberly,
>
> The Chugmeister General
>
> P.S. Tell NO ONE outside the office of this meeting's existence. Even though it's perfectly legitimate and it would be fine if you did.

Alternatively, you can ditch the fancy wordplay by issuing your invitations in a format that leaves no paper trail. These include:

- Oral, i.e. just telling people*

- Snapchat

- Mime

- Morse code

- Semaphore

- Smoke signals

- Skywriting (not great for keeping a low profile)

- Using a burner phone and voice-changing software. Your invitee will feel as if they're in a spy thriller!

- Having the invitation tattooed across your chest, then flashing anyone you want to receive it. You can always get it lasered off later.

- Rigging your invitation to self-destruct, *Mission Impossible*-style. Be careful, though: you don't want to maim the recipient, or get arrested for sending letter bombs.

---

* The downside here is the potential to be overheard. What if some greasy Poindexter eavesdrops on your invite and assumes it applies to him? For this reason, I recommend whispering behind your hand or, if you have time, inventing a secret language.

The first rule of Downing Street parties is you do not talk about Downing Street parties.

VB-K's Q&As

Throughout the book you'll find multiple-choice scenarios, designed to test whether you have the right mentality to host raves in the heart of government. Ask yourself WWBJD – What Would Boris Johnson Do? (Generally: have an affair, then lie about it.)

Question: A colleague turns down his invitation, politely but firmly stating that he doesn't want to attend a party at this point in the pandemic. What's your response?

Answer:

A) Accept it with good grace. You appreciate that not everyone's as cool and devil-may-care as you.

B) Eff that: you basically gave this goon a golden ticket, and he's used it to wipe his chocolate factory. Mount a whisper campaign in the office, turning everyone against him. He won't understand why all his colleagues are giving him the cold shoulder and will gradually become depressed and withdrawn. That'll teach him for not coming to your party.

C) Fire the guy on the spot. If he wants to be socially distant, he can distance himself out of the building. Oh, and make it clear that if he breathes a word about secret parties he won't be able to get a job licking stamps in CCHQ.

Turn to page 163 for the correct response.

SETTING & DECOR

—◆—

Now that invites have been sent and dates saved, it's time to think location. The wrong choice of venue is at best a buzzkill and at worst actively dangerous. I remember my good friend Icky Maxwell-Bloot once threw a cocktail party on an enormous bouncy castle. Inevitably, someone dropped a skewer, piercing the PVC and causing the entire castle to collapse. In the ensuing chaos, three people were suffocated, as well as five members of the wait staff. It was a complete disaster. And think of all those parties on the *Titanic*: the cringe must have been epic!

PICKING THE IDEAL VENUE

Fortunately, Downing Street boasts a wide array of spaces, meaning you're guaranteed to find one suitable for your event. Options include . . .

- **The garden** – A charming spot in summer – did someone say Pimm's o'clock? Just watch out for journalists with telephoto lenses, or any passing drones! And, if the garden is too Covid-safe for your tastes, you can always take the party inside afterwards.

- **Offices** – Number Ten has a tonne of these, all of which can house throngs of drunken revellers. Handy for when you have to explain these were work meetings. Other pros include desktops on which you can show your guests amusing cat videos, and filing cabinets, the drawers of which can be used as a vomit receptacle.

- **Boris and Carrie's flat** – For a more intimate affair, why not retire to the PM's own living quarters? You can be as loud as you want, and, if things need livening up, there will doubtless be some top-secret documents lying around. This venue is perfect if, say, you've just won a protracted turf war against the chief adviser to your husband, the prime minister. Now you've sent the baldy bellend back to Barnard Castle, why not crank up ABBA and let loose?

- **Press-briefing Room** – You may have seen that Boris spent £2.6 million of taxpayers' money on a White House-style briefing room for daily press conferences, then abandoned the idea in case they were rubbish. Fortunately, he did get some use out of it, using the hi-tech info-hub to screen the latest Bond film, *No Time to Die*. It could also come in handy for your party: the room, with its top-of-the-range audiovisual equipment, is ideal for a disco.

To help you work out whether a venue is suitable for the party you want to throw, here's a table of pros and cons to fill in yourself.

PROS	CONS

N.B. The above is included for the reader's benefit and *not*, as my editor suggests, to 'pad out an underwritten section'.

JAZZING UP THE PLACE

It would be social death to invite guests to a venue that wasn't perfectly decorated. Imagine if they suddenly found themselves in the midst of a John Lewis nightmare – it doesn't bear thinking about. That's why it's essential to bring in a swanky interior designer. 'But, Verity,' you cry, 'I can't afford that! I'm just a Geordie from Sheffield, working for tuppence down the chip mines!' Dear reader, you're not thinking like a posh person. The key to having loads of money is to never spend your own. If you need your party venue renovated, why not – say – get a millionaire Tory donor to chuck in a few tens of thousands? Sure, there are rules around that, but just think of your guests' admiring faces as they take in your gold Lulu Lytle wallpaper!

Now that your venue is spick and span, you can start thinking about party decorations. Given that the affair is meant to be secret, it's unlikely you'll be able to do anything too elaborate. (Wheeling a six-metre ice sculpture of Britannia into Number Ten would raise suspicions.) But this shouldn't mean a spartan soirée: go-to items like candles, tinsel, balloons and fairy lights can easily be smuggled on-site inside backpacks and briefcases. And why not get creative?

- Any official documents lying around can be turned into origami shapes or paper chains.

- You see someone feed the contents of a folder labelled 'TOP SECRET' into the office shredder? Free confetti!

- Put a lava-lamp screensaver on all the office desktops, then dim the lights to create a chilled-out stoner atmos.

- Staples are an excellent substitute for glitter. Just try to avoid throwing and/or ingesting them.

- Order low-ranking members of staff to pose as human statues. If they move, they're fired!

SECURITY

When you're hosting an ultra-exclusive and super-illegal party, the last thing you want is gatecrashers. Especially when said gatecrashers are almost guaranteed to be carrying miniature recording devices in their pockets. Luckily, another benefit of Number Ten as a venue is that it's on the most heavily guarded street in the country. Need security? Look no further than the officers of the Metropolitan Police. They're basically taxpayer-funded bouncers!

Now, you may be worried about the proximity of law-enforcement officers to your party. But don't be – these guys are one hundred per cent onside. You could literally be breaking the law in front of them and they wouldn't bat an eyelid. So why not offer vol-au-vents and cocktails to your loyal bobby bodyguard?

Even if the cops are forced at some point to acknowledge your bash, I'm sure they'll be sympathetic. After all, the Conservatives are the party of law enforcement (against poor people). Don't worry about your security detail getting sick, either. These guys are meant to take a bullet for you: they can hardly complain about a snootful of virions.

FUN FACT

You're probably aware that US Secret Service agents use special code names for the presidents they guard (JFK was known as 'Lancer', Obama as 'Renegade', and Trump as 'Mogul'). What you might not know is that UK prime ministers are also given code names by their personal protection officers. Boris Johnson has cycled through a number of these, including:

Schoolboy Tuckshop Manchild Lothario

Eton Flimflam Charlatan Vacuum

Weathercock Twat

NOTE ON HEALTH AND HYGIENE

Until now, we've been skirting around the C word. Not 'Conservative'. Or the other one people associate with Boris. No, I mean Covid-19. The 'Rona. The Wuhan Wonder. Over the past two-and-a-bit years, we've all come up with our own rules for partying in the time of Corona. In this writer's opinion, Covid is like HPV or climate change: the best way to deal with it is to ignore it. But, if you must be a wet blanket, here are some methods to make your party as Covid-secure as possible.

- Alcohol is a known germicide, capable of wiping out bacteria, viruses and fungi. It stands to reason that if you chug enough prosecco, you'll be immune to Covid. The trick to staying healthy is to consume the most alcohol you possibly can while remaining conscious. A bottle of vodka a day keeps the doctor away!

- Position a known loudmouth in every room so that their incessant blathering causes air to circulate. A benefit of throwing parties in Downing Street is that you have no shortage of blowhards.

- If your guests are drunk enough, it's highly likely that one or more windows will get smashed, thus improving ventilation.

- Find non-lame ways to incorporate personal protective equipment into your party. For instance, by staging an

Eyes Wide Shut-style masquerade ball (the cool kind of mask). Of course, your party doesn't have to descend into a satanic orgy as in the film. It doesn't *have* to . . .

- Similarly, you could throw a costume party themed around the HBO drama *Chernobyl* (amazing show, by the way – imagine if that actually happened!). This will allow your guests to attend in full hazmat gear, dramatically lowering the chances of transmission. Plus, they can do funny Russian accents and use words like 'roentgen'.

- The most drastic response would be to cancel your party and abide by the national lockdown. But, come on, what kind of rube would do that?

TOP TIP

More important than following health-and-safety regulations is being perceived to follow them. If you're worried about photos of your event getting out, hire a face painter to draw blue surgical masks on your guests' faces. This way they can drink, laugh and smoke to their hearts' content, all the while looking Covid-responsible.

Covid may be infectious,
but so is fun!

APPROPRIATE ATTIRE

—◆—

They say that clothes make the man/woman, and this is true everywhere, except perhaps a nudist colony. Even there, you're probably being judged on physique, regrettable tattoos, pubic hair maintenance, etc. The point is, appearances matter, no less at parties than more formal occasions. Each party is different, and there's no such thing as an outfit that works in every context. The same latex gimp suit that would be celebrated at Berlin's Berghain nightclub would raise eyebrows at a luncheon for the Archbishop of York. This chapter will teach you how to show yourself off to best effect and avoid any fashion faux pas.

DOWNING STREET GUESTS AND THEIR GET-UPS

The types of people you find partying at Number Ten generally fall into one of three categories. Work out which applies to you and dress accordingly.

1) Junior spad
Tortoiseshell glasses, lanyard, Charles Tyrwhitt suit, Oxford Union tie, floppy public-school hair.

2) Friend of Carrie's

Bold floral-print dress, Gucci handbag, rose-gold designer watch with vegan leather strap, discreet tattoo from that amazing week in Mykonos.

3) **Senior government figure**
Slumped posture, purposely dishevelled hair, shirt poking through open flies, lipstick on collar.

This third category may be seen as a new form of power dressing. Traditionally, important figures would wear expensive, well-tailored outfits to assert their position. But in recent years innovators such as Brexit boffin Dominic Cummings and MAGA raccoon Steve Bannon have gone in the opposite direction. To demonstrate the extent of their influence, they deliberately dress like a toddler during a power cut. In Cummings's case, that means multiple scarves, gilet over Billabong T-shirt and beanie awkwardly sitting on hairless pate. For Bannon, it means wearing two button-down shirts at the same time, visibly stained blazers and generally looking as though he just finished a month-long bender with Oliver Reed and Hunter S. Thompson. This sort of vestiary insanity is a smart way to establish dominance. Just make sure you're a rich white man, otherwise you stand a good chance of getting sectioned.

But what if your style doesn't fit into one of the above categories? Perhaps you want to make a statement, like Lady Gaga when she dressed as a butcher's window. On the whole, I would discourage people from sticking out like a sartorial sore thumb: the line between trailblazer and weirdo is a fine one. However, there is one fashion icon in SW1 who blazes his own trail without ever putting a foot wrong. Of course, I'm referring to Tory pin-up Jacob Rees-Mogg, who has kindly agreed to give us his personal guide to party apparel. Take it away, Jake!

Top hat

Monocle & backup monocle

Multiple cravats

Ten-piece suit

Silver-topped cane

STYLE TIPS WITH JACOB REES-MOGG

Salutations,

'Tis I, the Right Honourable Jacob Rees-Mogg MP. As the man bringing back nineteenth-century chic, one has consented to provide a rundown of what any gentleman should wear to a convivial gathering. Having little interest in women (beyond Nanny and, to a lesser extent, my wife), I shall restrict myself to advising on men's fashion.

The *sine qua non* is a fine suit, preferably from the same tailor who dressed your great-grandfather. Beneath this one should wear an undershirt, vest, knee-length underwear, under-underwear and, of course, a male chastity belt. Don't worry about putting any of them on: Nanny will take care of that. Once these basics have been attended to, one's mind can turn to accoutrements. Those illustrated opposite* are the bare minimum, so one may wish to consider:

— Cashmere-lined peccary leather gloves

— Mother-of-pearl snuff box

— Lorgnette

---

* I anticipate your query: Mr Rees-Mogg, why do you need monocles when you already wear glasses? If you need to ask, you don't merit a response.

— Opera cape

— Plague-doctor mask

— Umbrella with sword concealed in handle

At the same time, one must forever be aware of the fashion faux pas that will invariably expose an oik, pleb or parvenu. A gentleman never . . .

— wears a waistcoat the Wednesday after the boat race,

— adjusts his cufflinks in the presence of the Earl of Wessex

or

— sports a bow tie in mixed company *unless* one matches it with one's socks.

So there we have it: follow these simple conventions and you too can look like a Dickensian undertaker. You will be admired far and wide as the 'right sort of chap', the kind who gives his children proper names like 'Erasmus Pontifex Ignatius' and 'Septimus Otto Octavius'. Of course, you may feel that it's too much effort, in which case you are welcome to continue wearing your novelty T-shirt and urine-soaked sweatpants.

Yours punctiliously,

Jacobus Reesus-Moggus

VB-K's Q&As

Question: A junior member of staff turns up to the party looking casual and unkempt. This kind of slovenly appearance is reserved for senior types, ones with initials like B. J. or D. C. How do you respond?

Answer:

A) Let it slide. After all, the point of an office party is to unwind, not to stand on ceremony.

B) Take your errant colleague to one side and suggest, gently but firmly, that they may want to give themselves a once-over before returning to the party.

C) Deal with it Bullingdon Club-style: debag the rotter, then kick them out of the building to wander home in their Y-fronts.

Turn to page 163 for the correct response.

A successful party is 90% preparation and 50% spontaneity. (If you only give your parties 100%, I'm not going.)

WRAPPING UP

All right, let's take a breather and reflect on what we've learned. A Downing Street party is much like any clandestine debauch: the more you prepare, the better it's likely to turn out. This is as true for guests as it is for the host. You should spend hours considering each possible outcome and predicting the course of events, like that lady in a paddling pool from *Minority Report*. A useful exercise is to go through the following checklist:

❏ I have a politically advantageous guest list.

❏ If this gets out, the invites can't be traced back to me.

❏ Lulu Lytle has the venue on fleek.

❏ The bobbies on the door aren't feeling too observant, if you know what I mean.

❏ I've established a dress code, so no one's going to turn up dressed as Hitler or Mr Blobby.

If you can check all those boxes, your party stands a good chance of being a hit.

HOWEVER! Any series of social interactions is complex and fluid (do watch out for fluids). This means that, for better or worse, things are unlikely to go entirely to plan. According to heavyweight boxer and public intellectual Mike Tyson, 'Everyone has a plan before they get punched in the mouth.' Parties are much like boxing matches: loud, sweaty and liable to leave people unconscious. That 'punch in the mouth' may come in the form of disruptive guests, drunken indiscretions or an actual punch in the mouth. Throughout the next section, we will learn how to navigate the night itself and avoid too much unpleasantness.

Part Two

THE BIG NIGHT

REFRESHMENTS

—◆—

A party is like a planet: without atmosphere, it's deadly. But man cannot live by atmosphere alone. Your guests are likely to want to put things inside themselves over the course of the evening. These are what we professionals call 'refreshments'.

FOOD

'Food, glorious food,' sang the urchins in 1968's hit musical *Oliver!*, later the subject of a novelisation by Charles Dickens. And who can deny that food is an important – some would argue essential – part of life? That said, the role of food at a party should mainly be to serve as ballast, prolonging the period during which your guests can remain both intoxicated and conscious.

Here are some delicious hors d'oeuvres you might offer:

Bruschetta

Canapés

Caviar

Crackers with European cheese (feta, Gouda, Jarlsberg, Emmenthal, Camembert, queso, Manchego, etc.)

Gravlax

Mozzarella sticks

Spanakopita

That is, unless Brexit has continued to mess up food imports, in which case you can make do with Ginsters pasties and a multipack of Walkers Ready Salted.

Buffets

Unless you're planning a formal dinner party, *service à la française* is your best bet. Buffet-style dining is fun, unfussy and keeps guests circulating. Plus, it's a cinch to arrange a crowd-pleasing spread of finger foods. Just spend ten minutes trolleying around Marks and Spencers, with their vast array of smartly branded biscuits and classy crisps. Then again, I've been considering a boycott of Marks and Sparks ever since they renamed their Porn Star Martini. I mean, come on! Political correctness gone mad much? I for one will not be getting smashed in Regents Park off a 'Passion Star Martini'.

But I digress. Where was I? Oh yes: buffets are a fantastic option, but they come with their own set of challenges. Guests should observe the following buffet etiquette, no matter how inebriated they may be.

DO:

- Take small portions.
- Try to limit how many trips you make.
- Use a fresh plate when returning for seconds.

DO NOT:

- Lick every food on offer to determine which you want.
- Trip and face-plant in the potato salad.
- Perform obscene mimes with a cocktail sausage. If you do, don't return it to the serving plate.
- Start showing off how many chicken drumsticks you can fit in your mouth. (Twelve.)

A drawback with buffets is that they're very hard to keep Covid-safe. People crowd around, coughing, sneezing and spraying crumbs in each other's faces. But, hey, your guests knew the risks when they signed up. What are you going to do, drench everything in hand sanitiser?

P.S. I've heard whispers of more extreme forms of buffet, such as the Japanese *nyotaimori*, wherein sushi is served on the body of a naked woman. I'm not sure it'll catch on in the UK: it might feel a bit weird picking Scotch eggs off a lady, then dipping them in her mustard-filled navel.

Presentation suggestions

Why not use food colouring to dye your comestibles Tory blue? Or fashion the carrot sticks and hummus into an effigy of Michael Gove? If you feel like being particularly elaborate, you could even commission a cake, the icing of which forms a line graph showing the Covid growth rate. It's important to maintain a sense of humour (at other people's expense).

But don't get too bogged down in aesthetics. The aim of an office party spread is to provide hearty, unpretentious nourishment. Plus, chances are your guests will be so pissed they won't notice if you give them dog food.

VB-K's Q&As

Question: What should one do if a guest mistakenly wolfs down a slice of peanut-butter cake and proceeds to have a massive allergic reaction?

Answer:

A) Halt the party and immediately call an ambulance. Nothing is more important than the health and safety of your colleagues.

B) Keep the party going and try to treat the anaphylaxis yourself. How hard can this doctoring lark be, anyway? Tell the patient they're sacked, thus increasing the adrenalin in their bloodstream, or, if things get really bad, use a pen and straw to perform a tracheostomy.

C) Throw them out on the street. Tories believe in responsibility, self-reliance and freedom from the nanny state. If your guest can't handle a bit of anaphylactic shock, they shouldn't have been there in the first place.

Turn to page 163 for the correct response.

DRINK

Now we're talking! My grandmother always used to say 'everything in moderation, including moderation'. She also used to drink three glasses of gin for breakfast, but her point stands. If life is stressing you out – say you're in charge of the government response to a once-in-a-generation public-health crisis – you are well within your rights to indulge in a bit of C_2H_6O, aka alcohol.

For this reason, your selection of booze will be the centrepiece of any prime-ministerial party.

Our leaders have always enjoyed a tipple, from Herbert 'Squiffy' Asquith to Winston 'Blackout During the Blitz' Churchill. By caning it as soon as Big Ben strikes five, you join a storied tradition of liquored-up Liberals and wasted Whigs, of tipsy Tories and loaded Labourites, of sozzled spads and whips on the lash. Who could blame you for downing pint number ten in Number Ten Downing Street?

NOTE: you might want to avoid serving Corona. Not because it'll remind people of the pandemic: it's just rubbish.

Never waste a chance

to get wasted.

Acquiring booze

Taking a cue from politicians past and present, you should always have the following to hand at home and in the office: gin, whisky, vodka, brandy, beer, prosecco, and soft drinks such as lemonade, orange, apple and cranberry juice, and Schweppes tonic (only for mixing, though – this isn't a kids' party). That just leaves one essential tipple: wine. Naturally, you have a well-stocked cellar at home, but what about the workplace? You can follow the example of Boris's Number Ten and smuggle in a £142 wine fridge to keep things chilled for 'wine-time Fridays'. Or, if the fridge hasn't arrived yet, you can send a junior colleague to, say, the Co-op on the Strand, with instructions to fill a suitcase with booze.

The importance of said task cannot be overstated. Copious amounts of alcohol are required at any high-class function, as they take the pressure off guests to be charming or pleasant. A Downing Street party will include some absolute freaks, so social lubricant is a must. Put it this way: two of the coolest, most charismatic Conservatives are Jacob Rees-Mogg and Michael Gove. Imagine what the guys behind the scenes are like.

TOP TIP

In the nightmare scenario that you somehow run out of booze, bear in mind that many hand sanitisers contain a high volume of alcohol. Perks of the pandemic! And, yes, the British Medical Journal has reported that swallowing hand sanitiser can kill. But if you cared about what health geeks thought you wouldn't be hosting a party during lockdown.

Tory-themed cocktails

Spirits being an essential part of running a government, it's unsurprising that so many cocktails have been named for politicians. Here are just a few of those appropriate to serve at a Downing Street party:

- **The BoJito** – White rum, sugar, double cream. Served with ice and a single tuft of blond hair.

- **The Iain Drunken Smith** – A drink so colossally boring that no one can remember the recipe.

- **The Barnard Castle** – A mix of Newcastle Brown Ale, whisky and paint thinner. So strong you'll need your eyes tested.

- Last but not least, how about a **MAGA-rita**, in honour of Boris's mate, former president Donald Trump? Make Alcohol Great Again!

Ingredients for a perfect MAGA-rita

• **50ml of Trump-brand tequila**, the greatest tequila there is, and, believe me, I know tequila. I'm teetotal, but I know. We love tequila, don't we, folks? We don't like everything that comes from Mexico, but they can keep on sending their tequila.

• **25ml of lime juice**, which, by the way, the deep state and the far left Democrats don't want you to have. It really is a shame. They hate freedom and they hate lime juice. These are sick people, honestly.

• **A liberal measure of Cointreau**. And I don't mean liberal like Dr Fauci, who has been so bad for this country. I mean liberal as in 'a lot'. Come to think of it, why does liberal mean a lot? It's conservatives who like big things: Double Gulp sodas, AR-15s, SUVs the size of tanks. But fake news CNN wants you to think liberal means big. That's a problem and we're going to be looking at it very strongly.

• **Serve with a wedge of lime**, the most beautiful lime, everyone says so, and frankly these limes are being recognised more and more.

Toasts

The origins of the toast are lost in the mists of time, but it's a charming ritual that improves any celebration. Obviously, yours will be tailored to your own circumstances, but here are some useful examples that may or may not have been heard in Downing Street:

> 'To the prime minister, whose leadership during this crisis has been as intelligent as it has been compassionate.'

> 'To Boris, who cares about the nation as much as he does his own family.'

> 'To our health, and the health of all those we expose to Covid.'

> 'To our bosses, the Great British public. Just kidding: I mean the donors who bankroll this party. May they continue to win contracts regardless of competence.'

Dealing with drunks

One of a host's most delicate duties is handling those guests whose BAC has exceeded their IQ. This remains the case even at a Downing Street party, where any guest worth their salt is expected to get legless. The key is to identify who is merely merry and who is a legitimate threat to themselves and others. In cases of the latter, I suggest the following courses of action:

1) Persuade them to leave.

Given you work in politics, I'm sure you're a gifted and compelling speaker. Simply approach the offending guest and, in your most sonorous tone of voice, tell them to sling their hook or they'll be picking their teeth out of the carpet. Their angry posture will immediately wilt in the face of your sheer reasonableness.

Sometimes, though, such gentle hints aren't enough. Your guest may be the belligerent sort of drunk, the kind who prods you in the chest, or who implies they might tell the press about this little shindig. When that happens, a threat to boot them out in the next reshuffle, or to send their wife those photos of them with the researcher at the Grand Hotel Blackpool, should do the trick.

2) Suggest they go for a little lie-down.

If it's not an option for them to go home (perhaps someone else sent their wife those photos with the researcher at the Grand Hotel Blackpool), then persuade them to take a sobriety-restoring nap. The Cabinet Office is perfect for this, containing a long table on which they can stretch out. Should they need to take a midnight wazz, there are plenty of potted plants in the vicinity.

3) Make sure they don't get their cock out.

Given that most of your colleagues were in the Bullingdon Club or similar societies, they have an understandable habit of waving their willies around. While this has never been advisable, in the days of the smartphone it's a potential career-ender. Tell them to keep the Honourable Member in his constituency office, lest he end up on the front page of the *Mirror*. Especially if he's, as it were, standing for election.

4) Break up fights before they kick off.

I can confirm from personal experience that physical altercations are as common at Tory bashes as they are on Saturday nights in Newcastle's Bigg Market. Again, this is footage you don't want getting out. Imagine a slap fight between Sajid Javid and Grant Shapps. Forget Covid: anyone who saw that would die of embarrassment.

OTHER INTOXICANTS

Just a note* to say that narcotics should never be on offer at a Downing Street party. No Tory would ever take drugs, especially not a Class A substance such as cocaine. After all, they're fervent campaigners against drug use, supporting hefty penalties for possession. And if there's one thing Boris Johnson's Conservatives would never do, it's impose rules on the populace that they have no intention of following themselves.

Yup, rich guys who went to public school, then Oxbridge, then probably worked in the City for a while, wouldn't dream of racking up fat gorilla fingers of pure, unstepped-on blow. That's where they draw the line. They get sniffy about that sort of thing in the corridors of powder. I mean, power.

THAT SAID . . .

If there *were* drugs at your party, here are some tips on etiquette.

- Designate one bathroom for bodily emissions and one for, shall we say, negotiating trade deals with Colombia.

---

* A rolled-up tenner – LOL!

- Consider adding bowls of sherbet to the buffet, so your guests can claim *that's* what's caked around their nostrils.

- Offer guests a suitably shiny surface, such as your signed, framed photograph of Margaret Thatcher.

One good thing about Covid is that your guests now have an excellent excuse when they sneeze uncontrollably.

Ain't no party like
a Tory party.

VB-K's Q&As

Question: You're waiting for the bathroom when a guest emerges with so much powder on their face they look like a clown whose shift just ended. What do you do?

Answer:

A) Cast them out of the party, shouting that the police will be informed.

B) Politely indicate that they need to give their face a wipe, then suggest the use of stimulants is inappropriate in this context.

C) Ask them where they got the nose candy and if you can have the guy's number.

Turn to page 163 for the correct response.

ENTERTAINMENT

—◆—

In this modern world of zero-second attention spans, you can't expect your guests to just eat, drink and talk. If you want to stop everyone breaking out their phones and scrolling through InstaTwitBook, you'll need to lay on some entertainment.

MUSIC

As the famous bard of Stratford-upon-Avon (William Shakespeare) once wrote, if music be the food of love, then let's all eat some lovely music. Or something like that – I don't have time to look it up. What the baldy bore was trying to say is that music rules. A party without music is like a Bellini without prosecco, or a trip to Harrods without Daddy's Coutts card.

Crafting the perfect playlist

That said, even the bangingest party can be brought to a shuddering halt by the wrong selection on Spotify. Read on to discover the tunes that will get any Downing Street party popping. Remember, you don't want anything too heavy. Just fun tracks to distract your guests from Covid and the illegality of the gathering. I suggest:

'Breaking the Law' – Judas Priest

'Fuck tha Police' – N.W.A.

'In the Air Tonight' – Phil Collins

'Transmission' – Joy Division

'Infected' – The The

'Down with the Sickness' – Disturbed

'Still Ill' – The Smiths

'Fever' – Peggy Lee

'Every Breath You Take' – The Police

'You Take My Breath Away' – Queen

'Ventilator Blues' – The Rolling Stones

'(Don't Fear) The Reaper' – Blue Öyster Cult

Pretty cool, right? Nice and eclectic. Some people like to develop a theme with their song choices, but I just go for sick tunes.

It can also be a good idea to tailor your playlist to specific guests. For instance, if I were – theoretically – organising a Downing Street party that Carrie Johnson was to attend, I would factor in her musical tastes. Like Alan Partridge, Carrie's a famous devotee of ABBA, so they should definitely feature. At the same time, you must consider the sensibilities of the rest of the crowd. I wouldn't want to offend the Vote Leave lot with anything too European, so 'Voulez-Vous' and 'Mamma Mia' are out. 'Waterloo' would be a suitably patriotic compromise.

TOP TIP

If one of your guests has notoriously rubbish taste in music, do whatever is necessary to keep them away from the sound system. My number-one fear with any Downing Street party would be that Jacob Rees-Mogg turns up, commandeers the laptop and sticks on an album of Gregorian chants, killing the dance floor stone dead. Fortunately, this has never happened, as Jacob considers all mixed-gender parties to be sinful.

KARAOKE

Or should I say 'Carrie-oke', haha? Actually, I shouldn't: Caz asked me to keep her out of this. But it remains the case that a) Carrie does an electrifying rendition of 'It's Raining Men', and b) the Japanese invention is a boon to just about any party. That's why Helen MacNamara, the Cabinet Office's then head of propriety and ethics, had a karaoke machine brought in for the June 2020 leaving do of Number Ten aide Hannah Young (not to name any names). If at all possible, I highly recommend getting the Downing Street staff to belt out showstoppers, even if it means blasting virus particles in each other's faces.

Appropriate songs

- **'Mr Brightside', The Killers** – because Boris constantly looked on the bright side when refusing to lock down, despite overwhelming scientific objections. His optimism was such that, in December 2020, he waited until the absolute last moment before cancelling Christmas. Some people were salty about BoJo's indecision, which forced them to rip up their plans with less than a week's notice. But who can blame him for relying on a holiday miracle?

- **'bad guy', Billie Eilish** – ironic, because why would there be a bad guy in Boris Johnson's Number Ten?

Except for that creep Dominic Cummings, but Carrie dealt with him, the hairless Durham Svengali.

- **'Stayin' Alive', Bee Gees** – in honour of Boris doing just that during his Covid hospitalisation. It was such a shock when the news came through that he was ill, coincidentally a few weeks after he boasted of shaking hands with a load of Coronavirus patients.

Musical parodies

If you really want to go above and beyond the call of duty, you can alter the lyrics of a popular standard to reflect the occasion. For instance, during a Downing Street party, you might hear . . .

To the tune of Pulp, 'Common People'

I went to Eton with a thirst for knowledge,
Then studied Classics at Balliol College:
    that's where I
Learned to lie.
I soon became the Mayor of London
And spent all day with trousers undone.
I thought, Y*eah,*
Time for an affair.
Cos I . . .
Don't wanna live like common people,
Don't wanna act like all those little fools,
Don't wanna sleep with just one woman,
Don't wanna wear a mask or follow the rules.
That's really not my way
Because I am Boris J.
Provoked a bit of lefty fury
By giving funds to Ms Arcuri, but it's fine
Cos they weren't mine.
Was told I squandered public money.
But I just laughed and said, 'Oh, it's so funny
That you care.
After all, the public keeps on voting for me.'
Hence why I . . .
Don't have to live like common people,
Don't have to give a shit about the proles,
Long as I've got right-wing media
On my side I'll stay ahead in polls.

And what have I to fear
From that dreary loser Keir?
Swab your nose and wash your hands.
Cancel your vacation plans.
Spend all day inside your room.
Watch Mum's funeral on Zoom.
Christmas cancelled? What a shame,
Can't say that I'll do the same
Cos I'm out for a good time,
As I see the rules, it's not a crime, yeah.
I'll never live like common people,
I'll never face a single consequence,
Never fail like common people,
Never lose my job for an offence,
So I'll dance and drink and screw
Because there's nothing you can do.
(Instrumental break)
Laugh along at the common people,
Laugh along like Allegra Stratton might.
Laugh along at the common people,
Laugh along as they try to do what's right
And if you think that's cruel,
You went to the wrong school.
I wanna govern common people like you (×7)

To the tune of The Jungle Book*'s 'The Bare Necessities'*

Depend on herd immunity,
That fabled herd immunity.
Forget about the dangers that may lurk,
Cos we need herd immunity.
The whole business community
Wants us to send the public back to work.
Don't care if you're shielding, don't care if you're old.
Our donors aren't yielding, so do what you're told.
If you're infected, then that's fine,
Long as we serve the bottom line.
We can't afford to give you the bread
To stay in bed and stop the spread.
So you know what to do:
For herd immunity, let Covid come to you.
It's just like flu!
We'll go for herd immunity
Though Whitty says it's lunacy
To not lock down when people start to die.
But till there's herd immunity
We'll party with impunity
Although a thousand bodies pile up high.
We know it might vex nerds
Like the boffins at SAGE
But ignore so-called experts:
The virus must rage.
Don't give a single thought to the stress
That all this will place

On the NHS.
We can't be arsed to pursue the battle
Against Corona, and so the cattle
Will have to bear the brunt.
Cos herd immunity is cheap, it's worth a punt
And I'll be blunt:
Embracing herd immunity
Is good for Tory unity.
We need to keep backbenchers on our side,
And so with herd immunity,
A mad, destructive strategy,
We'll take this whole pandemic in our stride.
We'll take this whole pandemic in our stride.

DANCING

Okay, so you've picked your musical accompaniment and got everyone onto the dance floor. But the challenges don't stop there. Politicos and policy wonks aren't always blessed with an abundance of rhythm, so I've come up with some hints to get them grooving.

1) Lead by example.

The simplest and most effective method is to hit the floor and start shaking what your mama gave you. Don't feel abashed if you're not the world's most proficient hoofer. These events are most enjoyable when everybody gets involved, even those with two left feet. However maladroit you may be, you won't be worse than our beloved prime minister. I've seen Boris hurtle onto the dance floor like a blond bowling ball, sending pins (i.e. other dancers) flying in every direction. His uncontrolled drops, flips, lifts and turns have been known to leave a room strewn with casualties by the time he murmurs, 'So sorry,' and shambles off.

2) Identify the strongest dancers among your group and use them to encourage others to follow.

Attending the last few Tory conferences has given me ample opportunity to scope out the shape-throwing techniques of some of our leading politicians. I'm sure

Dominic Raab wouldn't mind me revealing an excellent breakdancer (his Worm must be believed). And then there's Theresa May, who does a hugely convincing robot, whether she's trying to or not.

3) Initiate a dance-off.

Those who work in politics are naturally competitive. By declaring a sort of low-stakes Tory *Strictly* (first prize is a fiver), you will motivate your dancers to up their game. Just be careful that the competition doesn't become too vicious. Displays of Latin, ballroom and freestyle can easily tip over into violence.

Controversial dances

While you should feel free to express yourself on the dance floor, remember that these are people you have to work with. No twerking, daggering or doing the macarena.

Dance like nobody's secretly filming you on their phone.

VB-K's Q&As

Question: You (a married, middle-aged man) notice a colleague (also a married, middle-aged man) dancing rather intimately with a pretty twenty-three-year-old researcher called Jemima. What's your move?

Answer:

A) Take your colleague aside and, man-to-man, suggest he reflect upon his wedding vows and avoid making any life-changing mistakes while in his cups. After all, he and Heloise are a wonderful couple, and the kids are thriving. Does he really want to risk that? Give him a bottle of Evian and send him home.

B) Take Jemima aside, warn her that your colleague has a raging case of herpes, then spend the rest of the night desperately trying to pull her yourself.

C) Do both of the above, and subsequently blackmail your colleague by threatening to send his wife the iPhone footage you took of him grabbing Jemima's arse.

Turn to page 163 for the correct response.

PARTY GAMES

It's the moment every host dreads: vino is flowing, beats are pumping and the dance floor is packed. But you sense a negative vibe spreading around the room, a certain lethargy starting to take hold. Perhaps your guests are tired after a longish day of steering the country through a pandemic. Or perhaps they're thinking about the likelihood that at least one of their colleagues is infectious. In any case, you need to do something, and fast. The answer? Well, I've slightly spoiled it with the heading, but . . . PARTY GAMES!

Who doesn't love it when their host yanks the aux cord out of the speakers and rushes to the centre of the room, brandishing Articulate or Boggle? Not every game is appropriate for a Downing Street party, though. Two Truths and a Lie tends not to work, as many guests find it impossible to limit themselves to one lie. And Carrie has made it clear that under no circumstances is Boris allowed to play Twister with female colleagues. To be extra safe, stick to the following:

Pin the tail on the donkey

In this beloved children's game, participants stand in front of a picture of a donkey missing its tail. One by one, the children are blindfolded and spun around, then must attempt to attach a paper tail in the appropriate spot with a thumb tack.

For my own parties, I devised a modern, politics-themed version: pin the tail on the spad. A senior politician has their tie wrapped around their eyes, and must attach the tail by thumb-tacking it to a hapless special adviser's buttocks. This twist on an old favourite is guaranteed to bring the house down, taking guests back to the sadism of their Bullingdon Club youth. Sure, the spads might yelp a bit, but they have to play along for the sake of their careers.

Never have I ever

A popular drinking game among students. For you Boomers out there, the rules are simple: you form a circle and the first player states something that he or she has never done, e.g.: 'Never have I ever made love to an orangutan in my mother's sitting room.' At this point, everyone in the circle who *has* made love to an orangutan in their mother's sitting room takes a drink. No judgement!

The game's a lot of fun, but you do have to be careful. I remember one instance where the first three statements were 'never have I ever cheated on a partner', 'never have I ever been sacked for lying' and 'never have I ever called Muslim women letterboxes and bank robbers'. A certain prime minister drank so much he nearly passed out.

Spin the bottle

Some may feel this is inappropriate in a world that's both post-Covid and post-MeToo. To them I say: lighten up! Where's the harm in harking back to the giddy, hormonal days of adolescence? I mean, apart from transmitting the virus, obviously.

Just because you're the Conservative Party doesn't mean your parties should be conservative.

PERFORMANCE

Men in politics tend to be enormous show-offs, so will welcome any opportunity to make themselves the centre of attention. Fortunately, a little bit of showing off can greatly enhance your party.

Poetry

Obviously less *Paradise Lost* and more 'there once was a man from Nantucket'. Boris loves writing limericks, like the one in which he called Turkey's president a 'wankerer'. This presumably wasn't helpful when he later became foreign secretary, but hey, it raised a chuckle. In that spirit, here are some poems I've heard delivered at Conservative Party parties (I shall keep the author anonymous – wink wink).

> What bliss to be white, rich and male,
> And from Eton College to hail,
> Cos you know it's true
> That whatever you do
> You're highly unlikely to fail.

*

> Some chaps are by scruples constrained
> And feel the law must be maintained.
> My personal view,
> Between me and you,
> Is scruples are for the weak-brained.

A BBC hack Laura K
Will parrot whatever we say.
If you just WhatsApp
Her any old crap
She'll tweet it the very next day.

*

Joe Biden, the senile old chump,
Has come down to earth with a bump.
It's taboo to share it,
But his only merit
Is being less crazy than Trump.

*

I must say, that chap Kim Jong-un
Looks like he's been having great fun.
He fears not defeat
And feels free to eat
His favourite desserts by the tonne.

*

Dom Cummings, the bald Machiavel,
Was feeling a trifle unwell
And so he set forth
From London, up North,
Where case numbers started to swell.

Although the chap really did mean
To fully observe quarantine,
He hopped in the car
And sped off to Bar-
nard Castle, on which he was keen.

Old Cummings, as you may surmise,
Is one of our most cunning guys.
When press got a tip
About his day trip,
He claimed he was testing his eyes.

Jokes

Everyone knows that Boris Johnson is hilarious. He's a legendary laugh, from his stints hosting *Have I Got News for You* to his 'satirical comic novel' *Seventy-Two Virgins*. Who can forget his classic gags, such as referring to 'tank-topped bumboys', calling Africans 'piccaninnies' with 'watermelon smiles', and – perhaps most sidesplittingly – making Nadine Dorries culture secretary. LOL, LMFAO and, indeed, ROFL. He's also a notorious prankster, such as when he claimed that 77 million Turks would flood the UK unless we voted to leave the EU. Boy, did we have egg on our faces!

It may be intimidating to make jokes in the proximity of a comedic genius like Boris, but it's nonetheless worth trying. As such, I've collated a few witticisms that ought to slay in Number Ten.

* Knock knock.
  Who's there?
  The Met Police.
  The Met Police who?
  The Met Police who are ignoring this illegal gathering. As you were!

* I'm not saying Boris is cheap, but when Lulu Lytle told him the price of that wallpaper he had to go back to hospital.

* How many electricians does it take to screw in a lightbulb?
  One, but we're not going to hire an electrician. Instead, we're going to give lucrative lightbulb-screwing-in contracts to an assortment of our friends, neighbours and cronies, despite the fact that none of them has ever actually screwed in a lightbulb. This will cost upwards of £2 billion and result in lacerated hands, a floor strewn with powdered glass, and a raging electrical fire.

Rap battles

With the possible exception of young, economically deprived African-Americans, the biggest fans of hip-hop are middle-aged, middle-to-upper-class white men. Inspired by Eminem in the film *8 Mile*, a popular activity in Conservative circles is to engage in a 'rap battle', in which combatants take turns to improvise aggressive and self-aggrandising lyrics over a beat. All you need is a microphone and a rap instrumental to keep the participants (and no one else) entertained for hours. I once witnessed just such a battle at a Tory Party conference and recorded it on my phone. I'm including a transcript, which you can read at your own psychological peril.

MC Gove: (*Spoken*) Hell yeah, it's Michael Gove, bitches.
I'm gone off this champagne, so let me step to the
mic and spit fire. We're back up in this thing, eh,
Boris? The big homies of the Vote Leave campaign.
£350 million a week for the NHS? Add that shit up.

> Straight from the streets of Aberdeen
> It's the most sinister minister you've ever seen
> Yeah, it's me, Michael G-
> O-V-E
> Give me a knighthood now, and an OBE
> Cos I've
> Had hot rhymes
> From school to Oxford
> To writing for *The Times*.
> And I wouldn't want to be you.
> I'll take you out
> Like I took Britain out the EU.
> Plus I left Sarah Vine.
> Now I'm single, so, ladies,
> Get in line.
> No Gove, no love.
> You've seen me in the club,
> Dancing like a madman
> Who's high on drugs,
> But I
> Don't mess with charlie: went
> Straight before I entered parliament.
> Was in charge of Education.
> Now you fools got schooled
> Just like the nation.

Jacob Rees-Moggy Mogg:

All right, Gove, you frightful cove,
Give me the microphone now
Cos I'm hot like a stove.
One of life's Ubermensch-es,
Lying stretched out across the front benches,
Here to give the straight dope,
Devout as hell, more
Catholic than the Pope.
All my skills are tremendous;
I read Thomas Aquinas
While you gawp at *EastEnders*.
And the ladies are receptive
But I'd never break my vows
Or use a contraceptive.
Rubbers aren't my style
Although I'm so very fertile.
When it comes to kids,
Boz and I are in deadlock,
Except all of mine were born in wedlock.
Check my family pictures:
Started with one, now we're up to Sixtus.

Rishi 'Rishi Rich' Sunak:

Yes, Jacob, we know you're posh,
But that's nothing compared to Dishy Rishi's dosh:
Wealthiest in the Commons
And, as I like to say,
Mo' money, less problems.
Rather I should say 'fewer';
Don't wanna sound like I grew up in a sewer,
Cos I boarded at Winchester,
Oxford, Stanford, became an investor
At the dreaded Goldman Sachs,
Then a hedge-fund guy, straight piling up stacks.
Worth two hundred mill
But when inflation hits
I make the public foot the bill
So just do what Sunak says.
Once I'm PM, I can cut my own taxes
Then I'll cut them more
Cos Rishi S don't give a fuck about the poor.

Boris 'The Notorious BJ' Johnson: (*Spoken*) Oh, er, crikey! My turn, is it? Yes, well, ah. Blither, blather. Gosh.

Now the main event, Boris J, of course:
PM, World King, hung like a horse.
Stand-up guy, can't tell a lie,
Cross my heart and hope to die.
We needed a leader;
I threw my hat in.
Thought I could get by
With some jokes and Latin.
Turns out it's hard.
It's not the nicest
Being in charge for a global crisis.
And sure I look like a slob,
But do you really think you could do my job?
Gove, you're a nerd, look at those specs.
It blows my mind that you've ever had sex.
Jacob's too weird – don't fancy his chances –
And, Rishi, something's fishy
About your finances.
You don't want the scandal
Cos this Johnson here's too big to handle.

DECORUM

—◆—

Let's be real: any decent party gets somewhat out of hand. We're talking tearful arguments, ill-advised make-out sessions, career-ending displays of depravity. These are all to be expected and, to an extent, welcomed. None-theless, there are lines that shouldn't be crossed, so here are some pointers on behaviour for both guest and host.

TABOO SUBJECTS

People often ask me, 'Verity, what topics are appropriate, or inappropriate, to discuss at a party?' To which I say: 'Sod off, I'm not about to give you a bunch of free advice.' Given you've bought this book, though, I'm comfortable telling you: the key is context.

Consider the context of a Downing Street party. Almost everyone there will be a member of the Conservative Party, and responsible for implementing its policies. As such, you should avoid the following – potentially controversial – areas:

Poverty

Unemployment

The cost of living

Homelessness

Welfare cuts

The crumbling NHS

Failing comprehensives

Mistreatment of refugees

Cronyism

Climate change

Bringing up the manifold ways in which the Johnson administration is making British life coarser and more brutal would be an unforgivable breach of Tory decorum. Remember: there's a time and a place for politics chat, and a party at Downing Street ain't it. For this reason, limit yourself to more anodyne subject matter, such as the weather (except where this overlaps with climate change).

If the person you're talking to brings up a spicy subject – Israel-Palestine, for instance, or J. K. Rowling – you should deploy a neutralising platitude, such as:

— 'Hmm, yes, that's been in the news.'

— 'It's all going on!'

— 'Why can't everyone just calm down?'

CONVERSATIONAL DOS AND DON'TS

Now that you know some of the biggest rocks to steer clear of, it's time to learn more about navigating the sea of chat. Again, context is everything, so for the following examples, imagine you're talking to your Guest of Honour, Boris Johnson.

DO:

- Compliment him on having secured the Tory leadership over such impressive candidates as Andrea Leadsom and Matt Hancock.

- Tell him he was one of the best *Have I Got News for You* guest hosts, up there with Rolf Harris and Adrian Chiles.

- Offer him reassurance that he's not totally ballsing up the pandemic response, and that all those old people would probably have died anyway.

- Ask him personal questions ('How are your kids?'), but not too personal ('How many kids do you have?').

- Slag off Rishi Sunak. Perhaps refer to the chancellor by a childish nickname, such as 'Itchy Nutsack' or 'Scrooge McFuck'.

DON'T:

- Refer to any of the instances where Boris has lied, cheated or otherwise disgraced himself. (I appreciate that's somewhat limiting.)

- Ask if he and Carrie got a pre-nup.

- Say that you were really more of an Angus Deayton fan, and wish *HIGNFY* had kept him on.

- Mention the words 'Darius Guppy', 'Garden Bridge' or 'proroguing Parliament'.

- Obsessively quote favourite passages from his very funny and clever novel *Seventy-Two Virgins*, in which he uses such phrases as 'a mega-titted six-footer' and 'as buxom as all get out'.

Keep calm and

Carrie on!

FAUX PAS

We've all been there: the party's going swimmingly, then you make a subtle mistake that sours the whole evening. Perhaps you laugh too hard at a self-deprecating joke, or accidentally empty an entire pot of fondue over someone's head. These tiny infractions are called 'faux pas' by the French (a famously polite nationality). So how do we avoid such social landmines, especially in the febrile atmosphere of Downing Street? Stop being so impatient: I'm about to tell you!

- Don't wear the following provocative items: EU badge, Labour rosette, T-shirt promising £350 million a week for the NHS.

- Don't accidentally refer to Carrie as Marina, Jennifer, Petronella, Helen or any woman's name, for that matter.

- If you need to do a massive, wheezing cough, make sure you do it in the face of someone junior to you. If you're prime minister, feel free to cough in anyone's face.

- Given your guests are likely to include veterans of the Vote Leave campaign, it would be a faux pas to use fancy French expressions like 'au contraire' and 'faux pas'.

- Don't obviously flirt with a female subordinate in front of your wife. Wait until your wife is safely out of earshot.

TOP TIP

It's considered bad form to surreptitiously take videos and photos on your phone of senior politicians in case they are breaking the law. If you must do so, don't sit on said videos/photos until you deem it advantageous, career-wise, to release them. That would be bang out of order.

DE-ESCALATING A FIGHT

We touched on this in the Drink section, in which I advised you to pre-emptively break up any fights. But how? Here are some tried and tested techniques for when two of your colleagues start squaring off.

- Appeal to the better angels of their nature. Just kidding! Spray them both with a fire extinguisher.

- Run to the sound system and start playing the national anthem. If the fighters are good patriotic Tories, they will be forced to break apart, place their hands on their hearts and start droning 'God save our gracious Queen'.

- Create a distraction. For instance, point into the next room and yell, 'Oh my God, is that the ghost of Benjamin Disraeli?' This should cause your warring colleagues to forget their *casus belli*.

- Step in and offer your services as an impartial mediator to help them squash the beef. Then, as soon as they've calmed down, have your personal protection officers chuck them out the building.

- Harness the power of chaos. Get between the combatants and start punching yourself in the face while screaming, 'I'm a bad widdle boy!' Your colleagues will be so confused that they'll have no choice but to stand down.

LET'S TALK ABOUT SEX, BABY

Hanky-panky. Rumpy-pumpy. Getting laid. Sex. Or, as the French call it, *'le sexe'*. Given the number of virile studs and ten-out-of-ten babes in the upper echelons of the Conservative Party, someone is bound to do it at your do. Here's how to handle any *in flagrante* incidents.

1) *Take preventative measures.*

For instance, put up large photographs of Piers Morgan throughout the venue, thus neutralising all sexual energy. Conversely, you should make sure any photographs or paintings of Margaret Thatcher are covered up, as they are liable to send Conservative men into a masochistic frenzy.

2) *Encourage your guests to use protection.*

By which I mean the protection of right-wing media, who won't report on the incident, even if they do it against the door to Number Ten.

3) *Make sure no one gets caught on camera.*

We all remember when it came out that Matt 'Shagger' Hancock was having a lockdown-busting affair with Gina 'hot under the' Coladangelo, despite being Health Secretary at the time. The CCTV footage of their canoodling, leaked to the *Sun*, is seared into our collective consciousness. Hell, I'm getting aroused just thinking about that display of unrestrained Tory eroticism. But, as horny-making as the video was, it provides an important lesson: disable any security cameras before the festivities begin.

P.S. People need to back off criticising my girl Gina. Let's face it: when a sexual colossus like Matt Hancock heaves into view, there's only so long a mortal woman can resist.

4) Whatever happens, happens.

Ultimately, if a pair (or trio, or quad) of consenting adults decide to get jiggy in a supply cupboard, there's little you can do to stop them. So just be chill. If you walk in on a pair of Treasury aides giving a whole new meaning to 'Eat Out to Help Out', you should smile and move on. If you witness a senior colleague wearing nothing but a blue medical mask, and not on his face, shoot him an approving thumbs-up.

VB-K's Q&As

Question: You venture to the designated cloakroom, only to find a couple of guests making the beast with two backs. Locked in coital ecstasy, they haven't noticed you. What's the appropriate response?

Answer:

A) Discreetly return to the party, banishing the mental image of their frenzied congress.

B) Clear your throat and say, 'Room for one more?'

C) Invite the rest of the party to come and watch. After all, it's more amusing than Jenga.

Turn to page 163 for the correct response.

BONUS CONTENT

An extract from Verity's upcoming erotic romance novel, *Fifty Shades of Blue* (Book One in the Naughty Tories series).

Chapter the First: Clap Cheeks for Carers

Health Secretary Nat Mancock glanced furtively out of the door, then closed it, his powerful bicep straining against a tight blue suit. Within seconds, her ravenous lips were upon him. It was Nat's lover, Tina D'Amato, pushing him against the door of his Whitehall office. Golden sunlight glinted off his bald spot as he returned her kiss with interest. At the same time, he began to stroke and caress her, his hands flopping against her back like dying fish on the deck of a trawler. It was very sexual. Suddenly, she broke away.

'Tina, what's the matter?' Nat Mancock enquired in a deep, animalistic growl. 'Don't you like the way I'm pawing at you?'

'Of course I do, darling,' she replied, 'it's incredibly fucking hot. But don't you think this is kind of . . . wrong?'

Mancock frowned. 'You mean because we're both married with kids?'

'No.'

'You mean because I hired you with taxpayers' money?'

'Not that either. I mean because of social distancing.'

The minister drew her into an awkward (but still profoundly erotic) little dance.

'Darling,' he murmured, 'I'm less interested in social distancing than social kiss-tancing.'

It was such a good pun that she had no choice but to launch herself at him, like a horny swimmer diving into a pool of pheromones.

Once again, his hands wandered from her buttocks to her hips to her lower back, never stopping for more than a second. Though she was fully clothed, she fought to stave off the inevitable orgasm.

'This is what I call being hard at work,' quipped Hancock. I mean, Mancock.

Mustering all the self-discipline at her disposal, Tina broke away from him once again.

'But darling, shouldn't you concentrate on supporting the NHS?'

He splayed his Gollum-like fingers over her shoulder blades, pulling her towards his beaming schoolboy face.

'Honey,' he said, 'the only NHS I care about right now is Nice Hot Sex.'

TO BE CONTINUED . . .

If you're E. L. James's publisher and the above wet (sic) your appetite, then hit me up! I'm more than happy to consider any offer in the high six figures. – VB-K

MISCELLANEOUS

—◆—

Okay, full disclosure: there was some shiz I wanted to say and couldn't figure out how to fit into the preceding chapters. Arguably, I should go back and adjust the whole structure, but who has the time? Plus, you can just call a bunch of random stuff 'miscellaneous', which sounds super smart.

TIMELINE OF AN AVERAGE PARTY*

No two events are the same, but a successful one tends to follow certain patterns. Below is a rundown of how a Verity Bigg-Knight party might progress.

NOTE: My lawyers have told me to specify that the following does not describe any actual Downing Street party. Instead, it is my guidance for future hosts, which embodies the spirit of such an event.

17:00   At the precise moment clocks tick over from 16:59, staff begin uncorking wine bottles and letting off party poppers. Forget family and friends: these guys live to get wasted with their co-workers.

17:41   Gossip is flowing as freely as the Pinot Grigio. Did you hear that Priti Patel is lobbying to have her own parents deported?

18:10   A conga line has formed, making further mockery of social-distancing guidelines.

19:23   A group of revellers break off from the main party in order to cavort and caper in the Number Ten garden. One of them starts riding around on a tricycle belonging to the prime minister's young son, shouting, 'I'm a giant! I'm a giant!' The tricycle soon collapses under his weight.

---

*   Not that any of my parties are average, haha!

19:50　Now uniformly red-faced, guests begin committing minor acts of vandalism.

20:00　Make that major acts of vandalism.

20:58　A drunk special adviser places a lampshade on his head and attempts to insert his big toe into an electrical socket. He is wrestled to the ground before injury can occur.

22:05　A cabinet minister seizes control of the laptop connected to the speakers. He switches the music to an instrumental version of Dr Dre's *2001* album, proceeding to rap over each and every track, repeatedly using a certain racial epithet.

23:20　The party is now an out-of-control orgy of pure Dionysian excess. Grievances are aired and shoving matches occur. Someone smears cake on a portrait of Alec Douglas-Home.

00:30　By this point guests are deliberately coughing into each other's mouths, just for the hell of it. One climbs on the table and moons the crowd, revealing a 'f*ck the poor' tattoo on his right buttock.

01:43　A senior figure attempts to photocopy his rear end, breaking the photocopier in the process. He is taken to A&E in order to have shards of glass removed from his backside.

*

Don't stress about following this timeline to the letter. For instance, the photocopier thing could happen earlier or later in the evening. The main thing is that it happens and everyone has a magical time.

*When is a party
not a party?
When it happens in
Number Ten!*

SPEECHES

One of the biggest dangers that your Downing Street party will face (apart from news of it getting out and demolishing public trust in government) is people making impromptu speeches. To a man – and it's always to a *man* – these politics nerds think of themselves as silver-tongued orators. Every one of them was in the Oxford Union and they've only become more obnoxious since. If any of them jump on a chair and start tinkling their glass, you must act quickly to save your imperilled party.

Options:

- Kick the chair out from under them.

- Set off a fire alarm.

- Start an actual fire.

- Announce that a call just came through from the Ministry of Defence: North Korea has successfully launched a nuke at Chipping Norton.

- Trigger a flashbang grenade.

- Ask them not to make a speech.

These solutions may seem a bit dramatic, but I assure you they're all preferable to Boris going full 'after dinner' mode.

DIRT AND GOSSIP

Not only are parties an ideal place to exchange goss, they also generate it. If nothing scandalous occurs at yours, you might want to take the initiative. Perhaps tell a colleague that their wife had sex with another colleague, while a third colleague watched from behind a ficus. Or persuade a usually reserved guest to roller skate nude into the buffet table. The resulting carnage will be the talk of the town.

Gossip isn't just entertaining: it's useful too. I suggest you keep a notepad and pen on you throughout proceedings, and note down any juicy developments. That way, even if you get blackout, you'll still have a reliable record for future extortion. Overleaf is a template journal, with gaps for you to fill in yourself.

Notes on party, __ of _____, 20__

_____ drank _____ pints of _____ and

_____ all over the Downing Street _____

_____ and _____ had ___ ___ on the

_____.

I witnessed _____ inserting several

_____s into his _____.

An inebriated _____ referred to His Royal

Highness _____ _____ as a '_____ ___ing

_____'.

_____ described his intention to 'have a _____

_____ with a group of _____ and ____

the Pope'.

PARTY FAVOURS

Thoughtfulness is a trait common to all good hosts, so why not send your guests home with something (apart from Covid)? Party favours should be presented in an attractive, ribboned bag and can range from the practical – lateral flow tests – to the whimsical – socks patterned with John Major's face, or pieces of the True Cross. A particularly painstaking host will tailor each gift to a specific guest. For instance, here is what I might give some prominent politicians:

- Boris Johnson – *Wine crates and acrylic paints, so he can indulge his famed hobby of making model buses. Which is definitely something he does, and not just bullshit.*

- Matt 'Handsy' Hancock – *Breath-freshening mints, extra-large box of condoms.*

- Dominic 'Megamind' Cummings – *Pocket-sized edition of Machiavelli's* The Prince, *coffee mug labelled 'World's Most Evil Genius'.*

- Priti 'Deport 'Em All' Patel – *Eye mask and white-noise machine (to help her sleep at night).*

- Jacob 'The Victorian' Rees-Mogg – *A new cat o' nine tails, for self-flagellation purposes.*

WRAPPING UP

—◆—

Congratulations. You did it. Bloody well done! After all your preparation, after all your anxiety and fervent prayer, a party has been thrown. And not just any party: a great one! You leave in your wake a scene of total devastation, like the Battle of the Somme, if instead of a battle it was an epic booze-up.

As you stagger into the waiting Uber and slur your home address, you feel a sense of triumph. You planned that party with a skill worthy of Verity Bigg-Knight herself. You created a mood of bonhomie. You subtly and expertly manoeuvred guests into optimal configurations. And you smartly sidestepped each and every social pitfall. A good time was had by all and there were absolutely no negative consequences.

Content, you sink into the plush leather seat and close your eyes. What's that? A tiny itch at the back of your mind. Is there something you're forgetting? Ah well, that's a problem for Tomorrow You.

Part Three

THE MORNING
AFTER

THE CLEAN-UP

—◆—

Oh God, your head . . . What did you do last night? And why is there a traffic cone, a half-empty jar of peanut butter and a live sable in your bed? You flash back to the mayhem of the previous evening. That's right, the Downing Street party! It was a roaring success, one that will live for ever in the memories of those who can remember it. But there remain some delicate matters to attend to . . .

LOST AND FOUND

A conscientious host will do a sweep of the venue the next morning. This goes double when said venue is the official residence and executive office of the First Lord of the Treasury. Be on the lookout for items beyond the usual party detritus. The Number Ten cleaners should clear up the empty bottles, torn garments and bodily fluids (they're very tight-lipped and have always seen worse). But after a really good party there are inevitably sensitive items that one should tidy away oneself. You might find, for example:

a set of false teeth

a pair of monogrammed boxer shorts

a prosthetic leg

an original copy of the Magna Carta

a thumb drive containing all the Whips' Office's blackmail material on MPs

an Infinity Stone

a blood bag (450ml, O negative)

a written confession from the Zodiac killer (you'll *never* guess who it is!)

Once you've flung all these into a black bin liner and stashed it in the boot of your car, you can start to think about returning them to their rightful owners. Often this requires some tact: no one wants to be presented with a pack of extra-small condoms and told, 'I'm pretty sure these are yours.'

HANGOVER CURES

If you're an ordinary member of the public, it's likely no one gives a damn if you get plastered on a week night and have to call in sick the next day. Alas, the VIP guests at your Downing Street party don't have the luxury of bunking off. They must attend their TV interviews and sessions of COBRA even when suffering from 'the brew flu'. A truly diligent host will share with them the following techniques:

H_2O

Or, as non-nerds call it, water. Basically, drink an entire bathtub of the stuff. If I understand correctly, drinking lots of water dilutes your blood, so the alcohol sort of gets lost. I keep my fridge stocked with Fiji, Voss and Mountain Valley Spring Water imported from the US. If you're strapped for cash, Evian is just about acceptable.

Breakfast of champions

We all remember it from our student days: fending off alcohol poisoning with a greasy burger or a filthy Maccy D's. You're more mature now, so after you get dangerously drunk, have a breakfast of eggs and avocado on wholemeal toast, with apple slices dipped in peanut butter for 'dessert'. This mixture of protein and complex carbohydrates should give you the energy needed to, say, conduct an interview with LBC, or field that phone call from Vladimir Putin.

Hair of the black dog

Here's a patented Tory restorative, dating back to when Winston Churchill boozed his way through World War Two:

Ingredients

Two measures of gin
Half a measure of brandy
One cup of pickle juice
Two more measures of gin
One egg, yolk unbroken
Five tablespoons of Worcestershire sauce
A dash of cigar ash
Seven strands of bulldog fur

Method – Set fire to the resulting concoction, then serve with olives and a miniature Union Jack. I've never tried this one, but if it was good enough for Winston – voted Greatest Briton on a 2002 BBC series! – then it's good enough for me.

Medical intervention

Down whatever's in your bathroom cabinet: aspirin, ibuprofen, ivermectin, Viagra. Remember, the maximum dosage on the label is just a suggestion. You may also want to self-administer an IV drip. There's a recent trend in Los Angeles for 'IV lounges', in which celebs like Rihanna and the Real Housewives pay hundreds of dollars to be pumped full of vitamins. If famous Americans are doing it, you know it's for real!

TOP TIP

A surefire method to ward off hangovers is to never stop drinking. If you keep your BAC above a certain point (0.10), then you're safe, sort of like the bus in *Speed*. I know what you're thinking: how can I maintain my buzz while I'm asleep? Way ahead of you. Just ask a friend to stay up all night, alternately breathalysing you and feeding you wine through a funnel. Anyone who isn't willing to do this is *not your friend*.

WHAT IF YOUR PARTY WAS A SUPERSPREADER EVENT?

Ugh, I guess we have to talk Covid again . . .

As much as we may wish otherwise, there's a chance the 'Rona will strike your party. These things happen when you ram dozens of people into a poorly ventilated space and let them drink and dance for hours. An additional health risk is that the event was full of Tory boys, whose tendency to bray, bellow and chortle has been proven to increase the rate of transmission threefold.

But, look, there's no point crying over spilt milk, or spread virus. My advice is pretend it never happened. Everyone should keep coming into the office, chatting around the water cooler, greeting colleagues with a continental-style double kiss, etc. You're meant to be in charge of getting Covid rates down: you can't admit to being some kind of pissed-up Typhoid Mary.

Rules are for the

little people.

VB-K's Q&As

Question: You've been infected by the severe acute respiratory syndrome coronavirus 2, aka Covid. You've done a lateral flow test and the lines are undeniable. No two ways about it: you're pozzed up to the max. You check your diary and see the days ahead are full of official engagements. What to do . . . ?

Answer:

A) Publicly announce your Covid status and that you will be self-isolating for the next ten days. Even if this raises suspicions about your adherence to lockdown, it's better than potentially passing on a dreadful disease to others.

B) Pretend you're not infected, like the survivor in a zombie film who's hiding a bite mark under their sleeve. At the same time, try to rearrange meetings and limit contact with others. And obviously, wear an N95 mask at all times. You may be bending the rules, but you're not a monster.

C) Screw that: you'll be damned if some piddling particles are going to throw you off course. You need to project health and virility, which you can hardly do sitting at home in your pants. So visit that school. Take a tour of that nursing home. Hell, go maskless: it's survival of the fittest out there.

Turn to page 163 for the correct response.

LOOSE ENDS

Worried some intrepid journalist might splash your party all over the front page? Don't be! The vast majority of UK hacks are firmly on the side of the establishment. Either they've worked for you in the past or hope to in future. So, if you've followed the advice in this book thus far, you can rest at ease. Yup, you're sitting pretty . . .

MORE CLEANING UP

◆

What the hell?! Despite your fastidious efforts in the last chapter, the unthinkable has happened and journalists are doing their jobs. With your secret party now in the headlines, how do you respond? The same way as other cool guys like Richard Nixon, the CIA and the Catholic Church: it's time to take charge of the narrative!

MAKING A PUBLIC STATEMENT

Denial isn't just a river in Egypt: it's also what you should be issuing at every opportunity. Deny, deny, deny to anyone who'll listen. They won't believe you, of course, but that's not the point. The point is to string this whole thing out until people no longer have the energy to be cross with you.

Emotive language

When reports first emerge of parties at Number Ten, you should publicly act shocked and appalled. Use the following to generate your press statement:

I am

aghast / annoyed / enraged / exasperated / fuming / furious / honked off / irate / peeved / pissed off / splenetic / vexed

at these reports, about which the British public is rightly

agitated / bummed out / dismayed / distressed / grieved / shook up / sick / tormented / tortured / troubled / unsettled / wrathful.

There will follow a comprehensive inquiry, and any wrongdoers will be

reprimanded / disciplined / sacked / spanked / imprisoned / exiled / put in an iron maiden / hanged, drawn and quartered / shot out of a cannon / called a 'jive turkey' / left to die in the infinite void of space / made to watch an entire episode of *Mrs Brown's Boys*.

Careful wording

While the natural (and correct) instinct is to burble a bunch of nonsense, be careful not to say anything that opens you up to prosecution. Ambiguity is your friend, for instance in phrases like 'as far as I know' and 'to the best of my recollection'. Even a seemingly clear-cut statement can give you wriggle room. Remember, Boris told parliament, 'All guidance was followed completely in Number Ten.' But, cunningly, he didn't specify that he meant Number Ten *Downing Street*. He could, quite accurately, have been referring to 10 Nameville Road, 10 Addressington Drive, or any number of Number Tens up and down the country.

Technicalities

Clutch any available straw in your attempts to argue these events weren't, in fact, parties. No, they were meetings at which no one had laptops, files or notepads to record minutes. Fortunately, there was a lot of alcohol, which famously sharpens one's memory, meaning that none of your valuable work was lost. There was an exemption for essential work gatherings, so *technically* – if you squint hard and turn your head sideways – you didn't do anything wrong. Obviously, this is offensive to anyone with a drop of common sense. But you're not really trying to persuade people. You're giving your colleagues a flimsy pretext not to boot you out.

Nuclear option: claim that you're in a committed polyamorous relationship with the dozens of people who attended your party and thus constitute a single household bubble. This might raise more questions than it answers.

SURVIVING A TV INTERVIEW

Paxman. Neil. Schofield. These are the names that strike fear into Britain's politicians. Unfortunately, if you want to defend your good name in public, you will have to go up against this kind of verbal gladiator. But take courage: by adhering to a few simple rules, you should be able to ace the interview, or at least avoid crying or soiling yourself.

1) Never back down.

It doesn't matter how embarrassingly shit your answers are, as long as you don't seem embarrassed. Say photos emerge of you and your staff participating in a conga line, Twister marathon and strip-poker tournament. Simply claim that these were vital team-building exercises. If Paxman/Neil/Schofield questions the wisdom of team-building during a pandemic, say that a pandemic is precisely the time to boost morale and increase workplace cohesion.

2) Gaslight the public.

A big ol' problemo is that everyone watching will remember their sacrifices and hardships during lockdown. Many will have missed out on major life events, and naively assumed that the people issuing the rules were also obeying them. The challenge, then, is to make the viewing public feel as though they're the ones being unreasonable.

To do this, adopt an affronted tone and suggest they misinterpreted the rules. When you said gatherings of more than two people were banned, you obviously weren't talking about office parties. The public could have had parties of their own if they weren't so dull and literal-minded!

3) Act dumb.

In politics, your goal is often to seem smarter than you really are: widely read, across your brief, in command of the facts. Right now, though, you want to come across as having the IQ of a houseplant (and a dim one at that). You see, your best defence is that you were at these parties by mistake: the 'Ambushed By Cake' stratagem. Paint yourself as a sort of Mr Magoo figure, constantly stumbling into what you think are meetings, only to be confronted with scenes of revelry. You would never knowingly break Covid protocol: you were merely in the wrong place at numerous wrong times.

4) Move the goalposts.

Interviewers will try to pin you down on the subject of resignation. Don't let them. If they ask whether you'll resign over these allegations, tell them there's no hard evidence. When hard evidence comes out, say you'll defer to the police investigation. When the police hit you with a fine, say that you never intended to break the law, and so on and so on, *ad infinitum*. Joke's on the interviewer, because you'll never resign, whatever the circumstances.

P.S. The pandemic is actually rather useful for TV appearances: when you wear a mask, it's harder for people to tell if you're talking out your arse.

The dead-cat strategy

Boris Johnson is a self-confessed fan of this technique pioneered by Australian elections guru Lynton Crosby:

> *Let us suppose you are losing an argument. The facts are overwhelmingly against you, and the more people focus on the reality the worse it is for you and your case. Your best bet in these circumstances is to perform a manoeuvre that a great campaigner describes as 'throwing a dead cat on the table, mate'.*

Even if people are appalled and disgusted, the logic goes, at least you've changed the conversation. A textbook example of dead-catting occurred in February 2022 when Johnson, on the ropes over Partygate, accused Keir Starmer of failing to prosecute Jimmy Savile. Bearing that in mind, here are some potential dead cats to hurl at someone taking you to task over your party:

- He once trained a parakeet to call him 'Big Boy'.

- He hurls *shuriken* (aka ninja throwing stars) at the postman.

- If he spots a small child reading one of the early *Harry Potter* books, he marches up to tell them Dumbledore dies. He then yells, 'Spoiler alert!' and runs away, laughing.

- He's spying for another country, but one you wouldn't expect, like Micronesia or New Zealand.

- In 2019, he was spotted in a Wuhan wet market, frantically smushing together a bat and a pangolin.

- He went back in time and killed the guy sent back in time to kill Hitler.

- I dunno, something involving actual dead cats?

Again, don't worry that every one of these is made up. Facts don't matter. All that matters is that people stop talking about Downing Street parties and start talking about parakeets/*shuriken*/Micronesia. In the unlikely event that your dead-cat strategy fails, you still have one option: blame the parties on Jeremy Corbyn. No matter how tenuous the charge, the entire British media will fall over themselves to attack that deplorable Communist.

VB-K's Q&As

Question: Beth Rigby or someone of that nature has got you on camera and keeps hammering you with questions. Sweat beads on your forehead as the contradictions mount and you realise no one is convinced. What do you do?

Answer:

A) Confess to everything, prostrate yourself before the British public and beg for their forgiveness. It's all going to come out anyway, so there's no point dragging your heels.

B) Keep brazening it out. If you slowly, laboriously repeat the same talking points again and again, eventually the public will get bored. People's attention spans are shot from social media, so they'll soon be distracted by an Instagram beef or the emergence of a new Kardashian.

C) Smile enigmatically, then, with a triumphant 'BWAH!', hurl a smoke bomb at Beth Rigby's feet. Once the cloud disperses, you're nowhere to be seen. In political circles, this is known as the 'Batman Manoeuvre'.

Turn to page 163 for the correct response.

BoJo bingo

This is a fun way to learn how to stonewall any question. Play at home by watching a clip of Boris being asked about Partygate and marking down when he says the following:

'We must wait for Sue Gray to issue her findings'	'I don't intend to provide a running commentary'
General Boris burbling	'What about Keir Starmer? I heard he had a vodka luge installed at Labour HQ'
'I wouldn't want to pre-empt the Met's investigation'	'In the meantime, we are getting on with X'

'I think what the British public *really* cares about is Y'	'I've addressed this point many times already'
'I have been entirely clear throughout'	'I look forward to addressing all of these issues in due course'
'I'm not sure I understand the question'	'I refer you to my previous answer'
'If Labour were in power, we'd still be in lockdown'	'I must say, you're rather harping on about this relatively trivial matter'
'It's important that all the facts are established before I make a comment'	*Pulls funny face*

Shamelessness is a superpower.

SILENCING POTENTIAL WHISTLEBLOWERS

At the same time that you're doing media rounds to protest your innocence, you should be ensuring that no evidence of your guilt comes out. As the media sharks circle, it will be tempting for your co-conspirators to break omertà. You need to plug the leaks and nip any aspiring Snowdens in the bud. The most obvious solution is to offer them a promotion in exchange for signing NDAs. Alternatively, you could dangle a recommendation to a posting in some tropical country with a very undemanding relationship to the United Kingdom.

If bribery doesn't work, try threats. You can even send them in the form of Thank You notes to individual guests. For example:

> *Dear X,*
>
> *It was splendid to see you at that <u>meeting</u> last Thursday. As ever, your wit and bonhomie were a boon to the occasion. Y and I really are your biggest fans, and would be devastated if something were to happen to you, perhaps as a result of you blabbing to some wanker on Fleet Street. But we both know that would never happen, don't we?*
>
> *Yours threateningly,*
>
> *Z*
>
> *P.S. In case it wasn't clear, I'm trying to intimidate you into silence.*

VB-K's Q&As

Question: You're getting blackmailed by someone who has a bunch of evidence about your party. They say unless you leave a briefcase with twenty grand in unmarked notes in St Pancras station, they'll go to the papers. Ball's in your court: what's the play?

Answer:

A) Release the incriminating info yourself. Someone in your position can't afford to be compromised, and if you give blackmailers an inch they'll take a mile.

B) Appear to comply with your blackmailer's demands, while actively gathering blackmail material on them. Once you have enough, confront them, establishing a state of Mutually Assured Destruction. Sometimes stalemate is the best you can do.

C) Have a quiet word with an old school friend who happens to be a senior figure in intelligence. Coincidentally, the very next day, your extortionist gets a bag put over their head and wakes up in an MI6 black site.

Turn to page 163 for the correct response.

TOP TIP

When desperately trying to evade scrutiny in spite of some pretty damning evidence, you will rely on two key arguments:

1) I can't say anything until all the facts in this case have been established (by which point, fingers crossed, some massive news event will have knocked it off the front page).

And

2) What happened was very unfortunate, but it's in the past, and now is a time to focus on all the wonderful things I'm going to do for Britain (to be determined).

If you can make the switch from 1 to 2 within a micro-second, and the media goes along with it, you should be able to scrape through.

UNEXPECTED CONSEQUENCES

—◆—

Uh-oh. You follow the playbook and deny your lungs out. It seems like you've got away with it. Then some little rat goes and leaks photos of you partying to the press. What now?

THE BLAME GAME

Ah, the blame game: as fun as Scrabble or Hungry Hungry Hippos, but with more potential to destroy someone's career and life. If you've been organising parties in Downing Street, it's safe to say you have a long list of advisers, spokespeople and civil servants you can throw under the bus. Simply force the unlucky sod/sods to deliver a resignation statement along these lines:

(Standing on front doorstep, tears streaming down face, as a thousand cameras flash.)

Thank you all for coming. I hereby take complete and exclusive responsibility for the parties in Downing Street. Yes, I did Partygate: it was me and no one else. I let down my friends and family, my country, and my God. Most upsettingly, I let down [YOUR NAME HERE]. [YOUR NAME HERE] would never have condoned these gatherings. In fact, [HE/SHE] doesn't even know the meaning of the word 'party'. I am therefore tendering my resignation and will now commit *seppuku*. As I draw my ceremonial *tantō*, I think we can all agree that the matter is settled.

If your chosen scapegoat needs a little help falling on their sword, why not brief against them to a friendly journalist?

Laura K

> Yep, turns out he was the ringleader all along. Furious when I found out. Obviously I had no idea these parties were happening.

> Oh wow! Thanx for letting me know. Will tweet out now xxx

You can also claim that your dastardly employees tricked you, and that when you walked into the room full of wine bottles and streamers you had no idea it was a party. You asked repeatedly whether this was all okay, and they assured you it was.

APOLOGISE WITHOUT APOLOGISING

When defusing the furore, it's vital you sound contrite without actually admitting criminal liability. This requires very careful choice of words.

- If in doubt, say 'if'. E.g. 'If anyone was offended by my blacking up and setting fire to St Paul's Cathedral, then I regret that.' Or, 'I'm certainly not unsorry if some people interpreted the media narrative in a manner that potentially suggested to them that something not quite ideal might have taken place.'

- While apologising for abstract things like 'distress caused' and 'perceptions of unfairness', also refuse to acknowledge that you were at the events where you were photographed.

- In fact, maintain that you are not at liberty to say whether you attended any parties, as they are the subject of a civil-service report and a police investigation. Journalists will eventually tire of asking.

Don't worry if what's coming out of your mouth sounds ridiculous to you. The fact is that you're speaking a strange language, similar to English but radically different in meaning. Call it 'Borish'.

What you say	Translation
I am mortified.	. . . that I got caught.
I promise to do better.	. . . at covering my tracks.
I want to apologise from the bottom of my heart to all the people who are justifiably upset and angry.	. . . that they were dumb enough to follow the rules themselves.
This incident has given me much cause for soul-searching and self-reflection.	And the conclusion? I'm great, and all you bitter little plebs should naff off.
I dearly hope I will have the chance to rebuild the British people's faith in me.	You fools! You absolute peons! *Obviously* I was going to do something like this. With all due respect (which is none), you voted overwhelmingly for a famed liar and cheat. It's like the fable of the Scorpion and the Frog if the scorpion had told the frog from the outset: 'By the way, I'm definitely going to sting the shit out of you, you green idiot.'

DEALING WITH THE POLICE

Of course, it won't just be journalists who ask awkward questions. If the boys in blue come a-knocking, you don't want to make a Cressida Dick of yourself. You need to be ready, so here's a practice police questionnaire, with evasive answers filled in.

OFFICIAL
METROPOLITAN POLICE
QUESTIONNAIRE

To be completed as soon as possible, whenever you get a chance, though we know you're very busy, sir, so we totally understand if you don't get round to it.

Provided it's not too much bother . . .

1. Reports indicate a violation of Covid rules may have taken place on ███████████. Were you present at said gathering?

Define 'present'. Also, define 'were', 'you', 'at', 'said' and 'gathering'. Once you've gone through the entire dictionary, maybe we'll get around to what I did or did not do.

2. Was alcohol consumed on this occasion?

Alcohol could be consumed on any occasion. How can you be sure someone in the room isn't swigging from a miniature bottle of Grey Goose hidden in their sleeve? Or sucking brandy through a long, flexible straw that runs down their collar, all the way to a flask attached to their belt?

3. If this gathering was for work rather than social purposes, what work was done?

At the time we were discussing potential changes to the licensing laws. In order to better understand the subject, my colleagues and I decided to employ role-play. By all pretending to be obliterated, we gained vital insights into how any changes might impact the public.

4. Did any of the attendees make physical contact?

Well, from what I understand of physics, atoms are largely made up of empty space. They lack hard boundaries, and what we call 'touch' is merely the effect of their electrons repelling one another. Therefore, on an atomic level, it would have been impossible for anyone to make physical contact.

5. Were any of the following individuals present?

I honestly couldn't say. Due to the stress of shepherding my country through an unprecedented health emergency, I contracted a rare condition known as prosopagnosia, or 'face blindness'. This lasted for precisely the duration of the alleged party. Luckily, it then cleared up 100% and hasn't bothered me since, kind of like Prince Andrew's sweat thing.

Many thanks for your detailed and thoughtful responses, which no doubt exonerate you in full, Mr Prime Minister, sir. You won't hear from us again.

Lots of love,

Your pals at Scotland Yard

But don't fret about answering your police questionnaire: you'll have a high-priced lawyer to help.

*The only parties
that should be illegal
are boring ones.*

Redact your own Sue Gray report

If things go very badly wrong, you might have to commission a civil servant to write a report. But never fear! You can always strike out any awkward findings.

Par exemple, with a few smart redactions, this . . .

> The prime minister was responsible for an atmosphere of rule-breaking and excess throughout Downing Street. Everyone involved should be punished, but, ultimately, we believe that the blame lies with him and him alone.

Becomes this:

> The prime minister was responsible ▮▮▮▮▮▮▮▮ ▮▮▮▮▮▮▮▮▮▮▮▮▮▮▮▮ throughout ▮▮▮▮▮▮▮ ▮▮▮▮. Everyone ▮▮▮▮ should ▮▮▮▮▮▮▮▮▮ ▮▮▮▮▮▮▮▮▮▮▮lieve ▮▮▮▮▮▮▮▮▮▮▮▮▮▮▮ him alone.

Now for you to try, dear reader! Below is the most damning version of the Sue Gray report imaginable: see if you can turn a smoking gun into a damp squib with as few strokes as possible. For this exercise, you will need 1) an extra-wide black marker pen and 2) no sense of shame.

INVESTIGATION INTO ALLEGED
GATHERINGS ON GOVERNMENT PREMISES
DURING COVID RESTRICTIONS

General findings

These gatherings reflect both a culture of excessive workplace drinking and a flagrant disregard for the rules. Particularly egregious was an instance in which a zebra was released into the corridor, where members of staff shot it repeatedly with paintballs. The guidelines our government set out for public safety were routinely broken, which was condoned and encouraged from the very top. This investigation concludes that those involved should either resign or be sacked, having demonstrated appalling judgement and little to no interest in the public good.

Correct response: strike out everything after 'general findings', up until the word 'good'.

TOP TIP

If civil servants start to complain about boozing in Downing Street, there are many methods to disguise it. Why not . . .

• Conceal miniatures in your ministerial red box?

• Use a junior colleague as a sort of alco-mule? Have them stitch a bottle of Wild Turkey into the lining of their jacket, then insert a straw. This way, whenever they whisper important government business in your ear, you can take a furtive swig.

• Decant that vodka into an empty water bottle? In the face of coronavirus, it's important to stay very well hydrated.

WRAPPING UP

—◆—

Phew! Sometimes the aftermath of a party takes more energy than the party itself. Relaxing can be sooooo stressful. But if you do find yourself constantly on the back foot, attempting to fend off Partygate allegations, my advice is 'keep calm and carry on'. After all, our system was designed to protect people like you from consequences.

Sure, there might be so much evidence you broke lock-down restrictions that the police are forced to give you a slap on the wrist. And sure, a handful of your already hostile colleagues might call for your resignation. But here's what's fun about doing the decent thing: you don't have to! Just hold the line and keep saying whatever's needed to get through the next five minutes.

CONCLUSION

—◆—

Wow, I literally cannot believe I've written an entire book! And I did it all by myself (apart from the ghost-writers who took over while I performed essential self-care). But before I break out the Bolly and book that trip to Marbella, I should get down a few final thoughts.

Over the past ten chapters (like Number Ten – clever, right?) I've made it clear that hosting a successful party is no mean feat. There are hundreds of little decisions to make, a thousand rules to follow. But the most important rule is this: enjoy yourself. It can be tough hosting, especially in the midst of a deadly pandemic. Still, you can't give in to the little voices in your head, the ones that say things like 'the guests aren't mixing', 'we don't have enough profiteroles' and 'this is not only a brazen act of hypocrisy that shows me unfit for office, but an active threat to public health'. Instead, you should remember three simple words: Be More Boris.

Alexander Boris de Pfeffel Johnson is an inspiration to all of us who truly care about parties. He's someone who will party any place, any time, by any means necessary. For goodness' sake, the guy nearly died of Covid! Lesser men would have taken this as a sign not to mess with the disease, or at least found their appetite for parties diminished. But not our prime minister. He heroically grabbed the nearest bottle of champagne and proclaimed that the show must go on.

There may only be one Boris, but that doesn't mean that we mortals can't learn from his example. The main lesson of this book, and of Boris's premiership, is that laws are open to interpretation. If you can explain how you believed you were within the rules, that's as good as not breaking them. I suppose what I'm saying is: nothing matters, LOL! So take a chill pill and savour your Downing Street party. Because, no matter how many things go wrong, you'll probably get off scot-free.

APPENDIX

—◆—

Social media policy

Ideally, your guests wouldn't upload any photos of your Downing Street party. But the modern world being what it is, we know that's unlikely. If your guest thinks the angle makes them look cute, or the lighting in the Cabinet Office is flattering, that pic's getting posted come hell or high water. In such cases, you may ask your guests to obey some platform-dependent rules:

Facebook – Do not tag into any photos the prime minister, members of the Cabinet, or high-ranking civil servants. That would be a public-relations catastrophe. Then again, Nick Clegg works at Facebook these days, so perhaps have a word with him. Nick loves demeaning himself on behalf of Tories.

Twitter – Journalists spend twenty-eight hours a day on here: tweet about the party and it's game over. If you must say something, make sure it's non-specific and couched in baffling Twitter-speak, e.g. 'tfw you're in the office and the prosecco hits different frfr'.

Instagram – Good news, 'Gram addicts: the tech nerds at CCHQ have invented a filter that removes anyone important from your picture. At the touch of a button, that drunken Boris can be replaced with a giant smiley face or a Minion. Even so, consider using the close-friends list or stories feature.

TikTok – If you must share images from the party, this is the place to do it. TikTok is dominated by Gen Z, rendering it terrifying to millennials such as myself, and utterly incomprehensible to Gen X and older. Almost every powerful media figure is in the latter category, so it's probably safe to post a video of you dancing in the PM's residence, or lip-syncing to P!nk's 'Get the Party Started'.

Glossary of Tory slang

If you didn't read PPE at Oxford while smashing pubs with the Bullingdon Club, you should acquaint yourself with these terms.

Oik – *Labour supporter*

Pleb/plebbo/plebaroonie – *An ordinary voter, the kind you deeply respect*

Buller buller buller! – *To be bellowed upon sighting another member of the aforementioned pub-smashing society*

Gak, chiz, beak, Chomsky – *Cocaine, which you would never take*

Pec – *Money, which you would never use to buy/take cocaine*

Yat – *Attractive young woman*

Squiffy – *Drunk*

Tight – *Drunk*

Blotto – *Drunk*

Seedy – *Hung-over*

VB-K's Q&As – CORRECT ANSWERS

Have you been keeping a record of your responses? Good. Let's see how well you did.

Mostly A) Oof. Sorry to say this, but your choices are dangerously naive. You're clearly a dull-as-ditchwater boy scout who has no place in the ruling class.

Mostly B) Better. You're not a total drip, and clearly have the right instincts re: turning a blind eye, exploiting weaknesses and putting your needs first. You're not quite ready for Downing Street, but could do nicely in a less sociopathic profession, like Hollywood agent or torturer.

Mostly C) Congratulations! These responses indicate you're a party legend, and display the contempt for bourgeois morality common to all great leaders. If you're not already prime minister, then you deserve to be.